CHECKERBOARD BIOGRAPHY LIBRARY

U.S. PRESIDENTS

The
United States Presidents

JAMES A. GARFIELD

ABDO Publishing Company

Megan M. Gunderson

visit us at
www.abdopublishing.com

Cover Photo: Getty Images
Interior Photos: Alamy pp. 9, 13; Corbis pp. 5, 22, 28; Getty Images p. 29; iStockphoto p. 32;
    Library of Congress pp. 14, 15, 17, 20, 21, 23, 27; Ohio Historical Society p. 10;
    Picture History pp. 8, 11, 19, 25, 26

Editor: BreAnn Rumsch
Art Direction & Cover Design: Neil Klinepier
Interior Design: Neil Klinepier

Library of Congress Cataloging-in-Publication Data

Gunderson, Megan M., 1981-
  James A. Garfield / Megan M. Gunderson.
     p. cm. -- (United States presidents)
  Includes index.
   ISBN 978-1-60453-452-8
   1. Garfield, James A. (James Abram), 1831-1881--Juvenile literature. 2. Presidents--United States-
-Biography--Juvenile literature. I. Title.

  E687.G86 2009
  973.8'4092--dc22
  [B]
                                            2008041627

CONTENTS

JAMES A. GARFIELD

James A. Garfield served as the twentieth president of the United States. As president, he fought for **civil service** reform. Sadly, his term lasted just six months.

Garfield was born in Ohio. He studied hard in school and later became a college president. He then entered politics as a member of the Ohio state senate.

After the American **Civil War** began, Garfield joined the Union army. During the war, he was elected to the U.S. House of Representatives. After resigning from the army, he took his seat in the House. There, Garfield continued supporting the Union army. He also fought for the rights of African Americans. And, he helped establish the U.S. Department of Education.

In 1880, Garfield was elected to the U.S. Senate. But before he could take his seat, he was elected president. Garfield took office in 1881. That summer, he was shot in the back by an **assassin**. Eighty days later, President Garfield died. He had devoted most of his life to public service.

TIMELINE

1831 - On November 19, James Abram Garfield was born in Orange Township, Ohio.

1851 - Garfield entered Western Reserve Eclectic Institute in Hiram, Ohio.

1856 - In August, Garfield spoke at his graduation from Williams College in Williamstown, Massachusetts.

1857 - Garfield became president of Western Reserve Eclectic Institute.

1858 - On November 11, Garfield married Lucretia Rudolph.

1859 - Garfield was elected to the Ohio state senate.

1860 - Garfield worked on Republican Abraham Lincoln's presidential campaign.

1861 - Garfield became a lawyer; he began fighting in the American Civil War.

1862 - On January 10, Garfield fought at the Battle of Middle Creek in Kentucky; in April, he fought at the Battle of Shiloh in Tennessee; he was elected to the U.S. House of Representatives in November.

1863 - In January, Garfield became chief of staff to General William S. Rosecrans; Garfield fought at the Battle of Chickamauga in Georgia in September; in December, Garfield took his seat in the U.S. House of Representatives.

1868 - Garfield supported the impeachment of President Andrew Johnson.

1880 - Garfield was elected to the U.S. Senate; he was nominated for president; in November, Garfield won the presidential election.

1881 - On March 4, Garfield became the twentieth U.S. president; assassin Charles Guiteau shot President Garfield on July 2; on September 19, James A. Garfield died.

DID YOU KNOW?

President James A. Garfield had the second-shortest term as president in U.S. history. William H. Harrison served the shortest term. He was president for just one month in 1841.

Legend has it that Garfield had an interesting way of entertaining his friends. For fun, he would write in Greek with one hand. At the same time, he would write in Latin with his other hand!

Eliza Ballou Garfield was the first president's mother to attend her son's inauguration. Also, the first elevator in the White House was installed for her use.

GROWING UP IN OHIO

James (left) *with his family*

James Abram Garfield was born in Orange Township, Ohio, on November 19, 1831. His parents were Abram and Eliza Ballou Garfield. They were farmers. James was the youngest of their four children. He had one brother named Thomas. His sisters were Mehitabel and Mary. Before James was two years old, his father died. Everyone worked hard to support the family. Eliza took over the farm and sewed for her neighbors. James's sisters learned to weave, and Thomas helped with farmwork. At 15, James began doing work for neighbors. He chopped wood,

FAST FACTS

BORN - November 19, 1831
WIFE - Lucretia Rudolph (1832–1918)
CHILDREN - 7
POLITICAL PARTY - Republican
AGE AT INAUGURATION - 49
YEAR SERVED - 1881
VICE PRESIDENT - Chester Arthur
DIED - September 19, 1881, age 49

8

James led the mules that pulled the canal boat.

washed sheep, and worked in the fields. Then in 1848, James left home to work on a canal boat.

The boat carried copper ore from Cleveland, Ohio, to Pittsburgh, Pennsylvania. It returned to Ohio with coal. While working, James often fell into the canal. He could not swim, so he almost drowned several times.

After a short time, James became ill and left his job. He returned home and was sick for five months. When James recovered, his mother urged him to go to school.

EAGER STUDENT

James's mother felt that education was very important. So, she was happy when James decided to go to school. To help him get started, she gave him $17. It was her life's savings.

James entered Geauga Academy in Chester, Ohio. It was just 12 miles (19 km) from home. James still needed to earn extra money while going to school. So during his first year, he did carpentry and other jobs. The next winter, he taught school in Chagrin Falls, Ohio.

James became interested in books at a young age. So, his mother encouraged his education.

10

No. 24
Jas A Garfields daily
Register January first
1848
Preface
It being New years day I commence a journal of the general events of my life. The object of this little work is to assist the hand a little every day in writing and also to assist in remembering events that are of some importance
Jas A Garfield
Orange Cuyahoga County Ohio
First Edition
Volume 1.
1848

James was an excellent student. At Geauga, he studied grammar, mathematics, and philosophy. James especially liked studying ancient and modern languages. He also joined a **debate** society and fell in love with public speaking.

At Geauga, James began keeping a daily diary. He would continue writing in it for 30 years.

In 1851, James entered Western Reserve Eclectic Institute in Hiram, Ohio. Today, this school is called Hiram College. At first, James paid his way by working as a school janitor.

At the Eclectic Institute, James was a devoted student. He got up early and stayed up late. And, he attended classes for ten hours each day. James studied challenging subjects such as geometry, Greek, and Latin. He also continued practicing **debate**. James became known as a good public speaker.

During his second year at the school, James began teaching. He saved money so he could continue his education on the East Coast. By 1854, James was ready to leave the Eclectic Institute.

In September, James moved to Williamstown, Massachusetts. There, he entered Williams College. Once again, James was a star debater and a good student. He was the leader of several societies, including a literary club. James also served as editor of the *Williams Quarterly*. Outside of school, he enjoyed fishing and hunting. In August 1856, James spoke at his graduation.

James's son Harry later became president of Williams College.

POLITICAL PROFESSOR

Lucretia Garfield

After graduating from Williams, Garfield returned to the Eclectic Institute as a professor. He taught ancient languages as well as other courses. In 1857, Garfield became president of the school. He was just 25 years old.

On November 11, 1858, Garfield married Lucretia Rudolph. Mrs. Garfield was well educated. Like Garfield, she had been an excellent student and public speaker at the Eclectic Institute. She worked as a teacher until their first child was born.

The Garfields had two daughters named Eliza and Mary.

They also had five sons named Harry, James, Irvin, Abram, and Edward. Sadly, Eliza and Edward died in childhood.

While at Williams, Garfield had become interested in politics. He soon supported the **Republican** Party, which had formed in 1854. Like Garfield, Republicans were against slavery. Garfield used his public speaking talent to support the party and its candidates in Ohio.

Garfield's five surviving children

Garfield was elected to the Ohio state senate in 1859. There, he fought to end the spread of slavery. In 1860, he worked for Republican Abraham Lincoln's successful presidential campaign. Meanwhile, Garfield had been studying law. In 1861, he passed the examination to become a lawyer.

CIVIL WAR OFFICER

The American **Civil War** began in 1861. Garfield was eager to serve in the army. So, he began studying military methods and historic battles.

That year, the governor of Ohio named Garfield a lieutenant colonel. Garfield **recruited** other soldiers for the Union army. They included many former students from the Eclectic Institute. Garfield was then promoted to colonel of the Forty-second Ohio Volunteer **Infantry**.

Garfield's men trained for several months. By December, they were ready to fight in Kentucky. Kentucky was caught between the North and the South. It had not chosen sides in the war. But the South invaded Kentucky to gain an advantage over the North.

On January 10, 1862, Garfield fought at the Battle of Middle Creek in Kentucky. The Union army forced the South to retreat. Because of the victory, Garfield was made brigadier general in March. The following month, he fought in the Battle of Shiloh in Tennessee.

That November, Garfield was elected to the U.S. House of Representatives. However, he would not take office until December of the next year.

In January 1863, Garfield received new orders. He was named **chief of staff** to General William S. Rosecrans. In September, Garfield participated in the Battle of Chickamauga in Georgia. For his courage, he was rewarded with the rank of major general.

Garfield and his troops won the Battle of Middle Creek despite being greatly outnumbered.

OFF TO WASHINGTON

In 1863, the American **Civil War** was still raging. Yet, President Lincoln hoped Garfield would take his seat in the House. Lincoln wanted men with military experience in Congress. So, Garfield resigned from the army. In December 1863, he went to Washington, D.C.

In Congress, Garfield served on the Committee on Military Affairs. In this position, he used his experience to help run the Union army.

Garfield was chairman of two other committees. They were the House Committee on Appropriations and the Banking and Currency Committee. He also served on the House Ways and Means Committee. In these roles, Garfield became a finance expert.

During the war, Congressman Garfield fought against substitution. This practice allowed men to get out of military service by hiring replacements. Garfield also fought for equal pay for African-American soldiers.

Garfield (center) *was chairman of the Committee on Military Affairs.*

After the war, Congressman Garfield sided with the Radical **Republicans**. They felt the Southern states should guarantee African Americans equal rights. So, Garfield favored a strong **Reconstruction** policy for the South.

Garfield also supported the **impeachment** of President Andrew Johnson in 1868.

Andrew Johnson was president from 1865 to 1869.

Johnson had broken a law. So, Garfield felt he should be removed from office. He was angered when the Senate voted to let Johnson remain president.

Education remained important to Garfield. So, he became a leader in establishing the U.S. Department of Education. He also

helped create the **U.S. Geological Survey**. And, Garfield became a **regent** of the Smithsonian Institution. In the late 1870s, Garfield became **minority leader** of the House.

Garfield served nine terms in the House. Then early in 1880, the Ohio legislature elected Garfield to the U.S. Senate. But before he could join the Senate, Garfield was nominated for president.

Garfield was elected to the U.S. Senate in January 1880.

SURPRISE NOMINEE

In 1880, Garfield attended the **Republican National Convention** in Chicago, Illinois. Garfield went to support **Secretary of the Treasury** John Sherman for president. Others also wished to be nominated for president. They included former president Ulysses S. Grant and Senator James G. Blaine.

Garfield gave a speech nominating Sherman. But in the middle of it someone yelled, "We want Garfield!" Soon, the delegates began voting. But after 33 **ballots**, no one had won. Then, 16

Wisconsin delegates voted for Garfield. Yet Garfield had not agreed to be a nominee. So, he jumped up and protested.

Even so, Garfield began receiving more votes. On the thirty-sixth **ballot**, Garfield was nominated to run for president. The crowd stood and cheered! Chester Arthur of New York became Garfield's **running mate**.

Chester Arthur became president upon Garfield's death in 1881.

PRESIDENT GARFIELD

In November 1880, Garfield was elected the twentieth president of the United States. He defeated his **Democratic** opponent, General Winfield Scott Hancock. Garfield won 214 electoral votes to Hancock's 155.

Garfield was **inaugurated** as president on March 4, 1881. In his speech that day, he promised **civil service** reform. In the past, politicians had rewarded their supporters with civil service jobs. This is called the spoils system.

Garfield decided not to reward people with civil service jobs simply based on their support. He believed in choosing the most qualified person for the job. At the time, the **Republican** Party was divided. Garfield promised to represent all types of Republicans in government positions.

However, many Republicans felt Garfield's appointments were unbalanced.

SUPREME COURT APPOINTMENT

STANLEY MATTHEWS - 1881

The president's decisions upset people who were hoping to get **civil service** jobs.

In his diary, Garfield complained that people were always pestering him for jobs. But this issue was not resolved until after Garfield's term in office. President Chester Arthur signed the Pendleton Civil Service Act into law in 1883. This law required people to take tests to qualify for certain civil service jobs.

Garfield defeated Hancock by fewer than 10,000 popular votes.

During Garfield's presidency, there were problems with the U.S. Post Office. For certain delivery routes, contracts were awarded to private individuals. Some individuals were trying to **defraud** the government. They were charging more money than their contracts said they could.

Thomas L. James

This became known as the Star Route **Scandal**. Star routes were named for the asterisk symbols used to mark these extra delivery routes.

President Garfield appointed **Postmaster General** Thomas L. James to investigate the problem. James and **Attorney General** Wayne MacVeagh soon proved there was a large scandal. The men involved went to trial after Garfield's term in office.

PRESIDENT GARFIELD'S CABINET

MARCH 4, 1881– SEPTEMBER 19, 1881

- **STATE** – James G. Blaine
- **TREASURY** – William Windom
- **WAR** – Robert Todd Lincoln
- **ATTORNEY GENERAL** – Wayne MacVeagh
- **NAVY** – William Henry Hunt
- **INTERIOR** – Samuel Jordan Kirkwood

ASSASSINATION

President Garfield died in Elberon, New Jersey, 80 days after the assassination attempt.

Meanwhile, Mrs. Garfield had become ill. She was recovering in Elberon, New Jersey. So, Garfield planned to visit her. On July 2, he arrived at a railroad station in Washington, D.C.

As Garfield waited for his train, a man approached him from behind. The man then fired two shots. One bullet hit Garfield in the

Charles Guiteau

back. The other grazed his arm. The **assassin** was Charles Guiteau. He was angry because Garfield had refused to give him a job.

As Guiteau fired the shots, he shouted, "I am a Stalwart! Arthur is president now!" Vice President Arthur supported the stalwarts. This group of **Republicans** opposed **civil service** reform. Unlike Garfield, they believed in maintaining the spoils system.

Guiteau believed the stalwarts would see him as a hero. Instead, he was arrested, brought to trial, and found guilty. Guiteau was hanged on June 30, 1882.

President Garfield lived for 80 days after the shooting. On September 19, 1881, James A. Garfield died. He was buried in Cleveland, Ohio.

James A. Garfield served his country for most of his life. He believed in hard work and the value of education. His assassination helped encourage civil service reform.

OFFICE OF THE PRESIDENT

BRANCHES OF GOVERNMENT

The U.S. government is divided into three branches. They are the executive, legislative, and judicial branches. This division is called a separation of powers. Each branch has some power over the others. This is called a system of checks and balances.

EXECUTIVE BRANCH

The executive branch enforces laws. It is made up of the president, the vice president, and the president's cabinet. The president represents the United States around the world. He or she oversees relations with other countries and signs treaties. The president signs bills into law and appoints officials and federal judges. He or she also leads the military and manages government workers.

LEGISLATIVE BRANCH

The legislative branch makes laws, maintains the military, and regulates trade. It also has the power to declare war. This branch consists of the Senate and the House of Representatives. Together, these two houses make up Congress. Each state has two senators. A state's population determines the number of representatives it has.

JUDICIAL BRANCH

The judicial branch interprets laws. It consists of district courts, courts of appeals, and the Supreme Court. District courts try cases. If a person disagrees with a trial's outcome, he or she may appeal. If the courts of appeals support the ruling, a person may appeal to the Supreme Court. The Supreme Court also makes sure that laws follow the U.S. Constitution.

QUALIFICATIONS FOR OFFICE

To be president, a person must meet three requirements. A candidate must be at least 35 years old and a natural-born U.S. citizen. He or she must also have lived in the United States for at least 14 years.

ELECTORAL COLLEGE

The U.S. presidential election is an indirect election. Voters from each state choose electors to represent them in the Electoral College. The number of electors from each state is based on population. Each elector has one electoral vote. Electors are pledged to cast their vote for the candidate who receives the highest number of popular votes in their state. A candidate must receive the majority of Electoral College votes to win.

TERM OF OFFICE

Each president may be elected to two four-year terms. Sometimes, a president may only be elected once. This happens if he or she served more than two years of the previous president's term.

The presidential election is held on the Tuesday after the first Monday in November. The president is sworn in on January 20 of the following year. At that time, he or she takes the oath of office:

I do solemnly swear (or affirm) that I will faithfully execute the office of President of the United States, and will to the best of my ability, preserve, protect and defend the Constitution of the United States.

LINE OF SUCCESSION

The Presidential Succession Act of 1947 defines who becomes president if the president cannot serve. The vice president is first in the line of succession. Next are the Speaker of the House and the President Pro Tempore of the Senate. If none of these individuals is able to serve, the office falls to the president's cabinet members. They would take office in the order in which each department was created:

Secretary of State

Secretary of the Treasury

Secretary of Defense

Attorney General

Secretary of the Interior

Secretary of Agriculture

Secretary of Commerce

Secretary of Labor

Secretary of Health and Human Services

Secretary of Housing and Urban Development

Secretary of Transportation

Secretary of Energy

Secretary of Education

Secretary of Veterans Affairs

Secretary of Homeland Security

BENEFITS

- While in office, the president receives a salary of $400,000 each year. He or she lives in the White House and has 24-hour Secret Service protection.

- The president may travel on a Boeing 747 jet called Air Force One. The airplane can accommodate 70 passengers. It has kitchens, a dining room, sleeping areas, and a conference room. It also has fully equipped offices with the latest communications systems. Air Force One can fly halfway around the world before needing to refuel. It can even refuel in flight!

- If the president wishes to travel by car, he or she uses Cadillac One. Cadillac One is a Cadillac Deville. It has been modified with heavy armor and communications systems. The president takes Cadillac One along when visiting other countries if secure transportation will be needed.

- The president also travels on a helicopter called Marine One. Like the presidential car, Marine One accompanies the president when traveling abroad if necessary.

- Sometimes, the president needs to get away and relax with family and friends. Camp David is the official presidential retreat. It is located in the cool, wooded mountains in Maryland. The U.S. Navy maintains the retreat, and the U.S. Marine Corps keeps it secure. The camp offers swimming, tennis, golf, and hiking.

- When the president leaves office, he or she receives Secret Service protection for ten more years. He or she also receives a yearly pension of $191,300 and funding for office space, supplies, and staff.

PRESIDENTS AND THEIR TERMS

PRESIDENT	PARTY	TOOK OFFICE	LEFT OFFICE	TERMS SERVED	VICE PRESIDENT
George Washington	None	April 30, 1789	March 4, 1797	Two	John Adams
John Adams	Federalist	March 4, 1797	March 4, 1801	One	Thomas Jefferson
Thomas Jefferson	Democratic-Republican	March 4, 1801	March 4, 1809	Two	Aaron Burr, George Clinton
James Madison	Democratic-Republican	March 4, 1809	March 4, 1817	Two	George Clinton, Elbridge Gerry
James Monroe	Democratic-Republican	March 4, 1817	March 4, 1825	Two	Daniel D. Tompkins
John Quincy Adams	Democratic-Republican	March 4, 1825	March 4, 1829	One	John C. Calhoun
Andrew Jackson	Democrat	March 4, 1829	March 4, 1837	Two	John C. Calhoun, Martin Van Buren
Martin Van Buren	Democrat	March 4, 1837	March 4, 1841	One	Richard M. Johnson
William H. Harrison	Whig	March 4, 1841	April 4, 1841	Died During First Term	John Tyler
John Tyler	Whig	April 6, 1841	March 4, 1845	Completed Harrison's Term	Office Vacant
James K. Polk	Democrat	March 4, 1845	March 4, 1849	One	George M. Dallas
Zachary Taylor	Whig	March 5, 1849	July 9, 1850	Died During First Term	Millard Fillmore

PRESIDENT	PARTY	TOOK OFFICE	LEFT OFFICE	TERMS SERVED	VICE PRESIDENT
Millard Fillmore	Whig	July 10, 1850	March 4, 1853	Completed Taylor's Term	Office Vacant
Franklin Pierce	Democrat	March 4, 1853	March 4, 1857	One	William R.D. King
James Buchanan	Democrat	March 4, 1857	March 4, 1861	One	John C. Breckinridge
Abraham Lincoln	Republican	March 4, 1861	April 15, 1865	Served One Term, Died During Second Term	Hannibal Hamlin, Andrew Johnson
Andrew Johnson	Democrat	April 15, 1865	March 4, 1869	Completed Lincoln's Second Term	Office Vacant
Ulysses S. Grant	Republican	March 4, 1869	March 4, 1877	Two	Schuyler Colfax, Henry Wilson
Rutherford B. Hayes	Republican	March 3, 1877	March 4, 1881	One	William A. Wheeler
James A. Garfield	Republican	March 4, 1881	September 19, 1881	Died During First Term	Chester Arthur
Chester Arthur	Republican	September 20, 1881	March 4, 1885	Completed Garfield's Term	Office Vacant
Grover Cleveland	Democrat	March 4, 1885	March 4, 1889	One	Thomas A. Hendricks
Benjamin Harrison	Republican	March 4, 1889	March 4, 1893	One	Levi P. Morton
Grover Cleveland	Democrat	March 4, 1893	March 4, 1897	One	Adlai E. Stevenson
William McKinley	Republican	March 4, 1897	September 14, 1901	Served One Term, Died During Second Term	Garret A. Hobart, Theodore Roosevelt

PRESIDENTS 13–25, 1850–1901

PRESIDENT	PARTY	TOOK OFFICE	LEFT OFFICE	TERMS SERVED	VICE PRESIDENT
Theodore Roosevelt	Republican	September 14, 1901	March 4, 1909	Completed McKinley's Second Term, Served One Term	Office Vacant, Charles Fairbanks
William Taft	Republican	March 4, 1909	March 4, 1913	One	James S. Sherman
Woodrow Wilson	Democrat	March 4, 1913	March 4, 1921	Two	Thomas R. Marshall
Warren G. Harding	Republican	March 4, 1921	August 2, 1923	Died During First Term	Calvin Coolidge
Calvin Coolidge	Republican	August 3, 1923	March 4, 1929	Completed Harding's Term, Served One Term	Office Vacant, Charles Dawes
Herbert Hoover	Republican	March 4, 1929	March 4, 1933	One	Charles Curtis
Franklin D. Roosevelt	Democrat	March 4, 1933	April 12, 1945	Served Three Terms, Died During Fourth Term	John Nance Garner, Henry A. Wallace, Harry S. Truman
Harry S. Truman	Democrat	April 12, 1945	January 20, 1953	Completed Roosevelt's Fourth Term, Served One Term	Office Vacant, Alben Barkley
Dwight D. Eisenhower	Republican	January 20, 1953	January 20, 1961	Two	Richard Nixon
John F. Kennedy	Democrat	January 20, 1961	November 22, 1963	Died During First Term	Lyndon B. Johnson
Lyndon B. Johnson	Democrat	November 22, 1963	January 20, 1969	Completed Kennedy's Term, Served One Term	Office Vacant, Hubert H. Humphrey
Richard Nixon	Republican	January 20, 1969	August 9, 1974	Completed First Term, Resigned During Second Term	Spiro T. Agnew, Gerald Ford

PRESIDENT	PARTY	TOOK OFFICE	LEFT OFFICE	TERMS SERVED	VICE PRESIDENT
Gerald Ford	Republican	August 9, 1974	January 20, 1977	Completed Nixon's Second Term	Nelson A. Rockefeller
Jimmy Carter	Democrat	January 20, 1977	January 20, 1981	One	Walter Mondale
Ronald Reagan	Republican	January 20, 1981	January 20, 1989	Two	George H.W. Bush
George H.W. Bush	Republican	January 20, 1989	January 20, 1993	One	Dan Quayle
Bill Clinton	Democrat	January 20, 1993	January 20, 2001	Two	Al Gore
George W. Bush	Republican	January 20, 2001	January 20, 2009	Two	Dick Cheney
Barack Obama	Democrat	January 20, 2009			Joe Biden

"Freedom can never yield its fullness of blessings so long as the law or its administration places the smallest obstacle in the pathway of any virtuous citizen." James A. Garfield

WRITE TO THE PRESIDENT

You may write to the president at:

**The White House
1600 Pennsylvania Avenue NW
Washington, DC 20500**

You may e-mail the president at:
comments@whitehouse.gov

GLOSSARY

assassin - someone who murders a very important person, usually for political reasons. An assassination is the act of doing this.

attorney general - the chief law officer of a national or state government.

ballot - a vote. It is also a piece of paper used to cast a vote.

chief of staff - the officer with the highest rank who advises a commander.

civil service - the part of the government that is responsible for matters not covered by the military, the courts, or the law.

civil war - a war between groups in the same country. The United States of America and the Confederate States of America fought a civil war from 1861 to 1865.

debate - a contest in which two sides argue for or against something.

defraud - to take something away from someone by trickery or deception.

Democrat - a member of the Democratic political party. When James A. Garfield was president, Democrats supported farmers and landowners.

impeach - to charge a public official with misconduct in office.

inaugurate (ih-NAW-gyuh-rayt) - to swear into a political office.

infantry - soldiers trained and organized to fight on foot.

minority leader - the leader of a party that does not have the greatest number of votes in a legislative body, such as the U.S. House of Representatives.

postmaster general - an official in charge of the U.S. Postal Service.

Reconstruction - the period after the American Civil War when laws were passed to help the Southern states rebuild and return to the Union.

recruit - to get someone to join a group. A person who is recruited is also called a recruit.

regent - a member of a governing board.

Republican - a member of the Republican political party. When James A. Garfield was president, Republicans supported business and strong government.

Republican National Convention - a national meeting held every four years during which the Republican Party chooses its candidates for president and vice president.

running mate - a candidate running for a lower-rank position on an election ticket, especially the candidate for vice president.

scandal - an action that shocks people and disgraces those connected with it.

secretary of the treasury - a member of the president's cabinet that heads the U.S. Department of the Treasury. The secretary advises the president on financial policies and reports to Congress on the nation's finances. The secretary of the treasury is the U.S. government's chief financial officer.

U.S. Geological Survey - a government agency within the U.S. Department of the Interior that studies public lands and offshore areas. Its research includes the quality and quantity of resources in these areas.

WEB SITES

To learn more about James A. Garfield, visit ABDO Publishing Company on the World Wide Web at **www.abdopublishing.com**. Web sites about James A. Garfield are featured on our Book Links page. These links are routinely monitored and updated to provide the most current information available.

INDEX